AWESOME
SPINNER
SKILLS

AWESOME
SPINNER
SKILLS

CONTENTS

© 2017 Weldon Owen LTD
An imprint of Kings Road Publishing
Part of Bonnier Publishing
Suite 3.08 The Plaza, 535 King's Road,
London SW10 0SZ, UK
www. bonnierpublishing.co.uk

Publisher Donna Gregory
Project Editor: Matt Yeo
Author: Laura Baker
Designer/Illustrator: Jeannette O'Toole

The information in this book has been carefully researched, and every reasonable effort
has been made to ensure its accuracy. Instructions should be followed carefully and no
tricks should be attempted near breakable objects, around animals or people who could
be hurt. You are solely responsible for taking any and all reasonable and necessary
precautions when performing the activities detailed in its pages.

Certain photographs used in this publication are used by license or permission from the
owner thereof, or are otherwise publicly available. This publication is not endorsed by
any person or entity appearing herein. Any product names, logos, brands or trademarks
featured or referred to in the publication are the property of their respective trademark
owners.

ISBN: 978-1-7834-2503-7

Printed in the UK

10 9 8 7 6 5 4 3 2 1

ADVANCED SKILLS

SPINNING WITH PROPS

HACKS AND MODS

OTHER DISTRACTION DEVICES

OTHER RELAXATION TECHNIQUES

WHAT IS A FIDGET SPINNER?

What is a fidget spinner? Only the most awesome gadget ever! If you're a pen clicker or a coin spinner, a finger tapper or a nail biter, you can take your fidgeting to the next level with these sleek spinners and calm those restless hands.

You don't even need to be a fidgeter by nature to get something out of this gizmo. Join in the craze and try out (or show off!) some super-spinning skills.

Fidget spinners are cleverly weighted with bearings to provide a perfect and near-silent spin. They can be made from plastic, metal or other materials and come in all sorts of shapes, designs and colours.

BEARING

Whatever the style, they're seriously addictive!

WHAT CAN A SPINNER DO FOR YOU?

Fidget spinners are powerful little things. They can help fidgeters and non-fidgeters alike is so many ways.

The fidget spinner was invented in the 1990s to help people focus, by releasing their nervous energy through fidgeting. Since then, the spinners, and other devices like them, have evolved to become a super-popular toy, gadget and challenge.

FIDGET SPINNERS CAN:

1 Relieve stress

2 Reduce other types of fidgeting

3

Focus your mind

4

Act as a release mechanism

5 Develop motor skills

6

Challenge you with tricks you won't stop trying until you master!

WHAT CAN YOU DO WITH A SPINNER?

You may be perfectly happy with straightforward fidgeting. Fiddle with the toy and get used to the feel of it in your hands. Use it to keep your hands busy, all while focusing on other things. Try out the basic challenges in this book to get started.

Or, you may be a fancy-pants, flashy fidgeter who wants to super-charge your fidget-spinning skills. See if you can master the trickiest of tricks and stunts in the advanced section of this book, but be careful: choose an open space and make sure you work up to this level. Spinning can be a dangerous sport if you start tossing before you're ready. As they say, practice makes perfect!

Track your tricks progress with the chart at the back of the book. Tick tricks as you master them, and add in your own stunt inventions too.

Now go on, get spinning!

ALL SHAPES
WELCOME

Fidget spinners come in a huge range of shapes and styles. The most common has three spokes, but fidget-spinner style has exploded and you can find round, square, tri, quad – even six spokes if you want to go that far. Pick the one you like best!

WHAT A FEELING!

As more and more people have started producing spinners, the material has varied hugely. Whether it's plastic, metal, wood or something else, what it's made of makes a difference on grip and spin. It's all about finding what works for you.

METAL

Metal spinners are heavy and smooth. The heavier weight gives them a strong spin. Just remember, the heavier you go, the less pocket-friendly they are!

LIGHT PLASTIC

Lighter plastic spinners are safer for younger users and getting started. However, their lighter weight means they won't have as strong a weighted spin.

HARD PLASTIC

Hard plastic spinners with metal bearings are very popular. These spinners aren't too heavy or too light and can be seriously good at spinning. They either have a smooth finish, or a bit of texture, which helps with grip.

HOMEMADE

Some people even make home-made wooden spinners. These can vary in roughness and smoothness, weight and shape.

ONE-HANDED PINCH GRIP SPIN

This is one of the very first tricks to learn – you'll find yourself trying it without even thinking! Master this skill to get to know the feel of the spinner in your hands.

INDEX FINGER

1

Hold the spinner in its centre, with your index finger on the top and your thumb on the bottom.

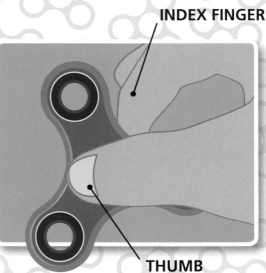

THUMB

KNOW YOUR HAND

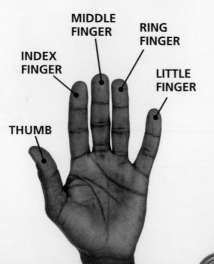

MIDDLE FINGER

RING FINGER

INDEX FINGER

LITTLE FINGER

THUMB

2

Place your middle finger of the same hand between the spinner's spokes (or on the edge for a round spinner).

3

Move your middle finger towards you very slightly and then flick it the opposite way. This should set your spinner spinning.

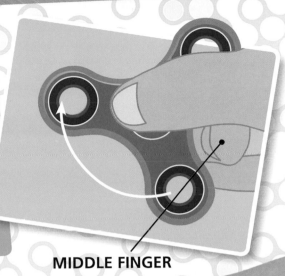

MIDDLE FINGER

4

Continue using your middle finger to gently stop and start the spinner. Hone your technique or just fidget like this for hours and hours!

TOP SPIN TIP
Swap your index and middle fingers if you find you get a better spin and hold that way.

FINGER PAD
BALANCE

This isn't just spinning any more. Progress from simple spinning to impressive balancing with this little trick.

1

Hold the spinner horizontally by its centre, with your thumb on the top and index finger on the bottom.

2

Set the spinner spinning, flicking it with your middle finger of the hand holding the spinner or your index finger of the other hand.

18

3

Slowly lift your thumb off the spinner. The spinner should now be spinning and balancing on your index finger only.

4

Try moving your hand up and down to show off your balance.

TOP SPIN TIP

Tilt and adjust your finger ever so slightly to find the perfect balance point.

FINGERTIP BALANCE

Look a whole lot more pro just by going from finger pad to fingertip. Whoa, skills!

1 Hold the spinner horizontally by its centre, with your thumb on the top and index finger flat on the bottom.

2 Bend your index finger so the fingertip rather than the pad of your finger is touching the spinner's centre piece.

3 Set the spinner spinning, flicking it with your middle finger of the hand holding the spinner or your index finger of the other hand.

4

Slowly lift your thumb off the spinner. The spinner should now be spinning and balancing on your fingertip only.

TOP SPIN TIP

You can support your index finger with the middle finger of the same hand while you get used to this trick.

FINGER TO THUMB TRANSFER

Perform a finger pad or fingertip balance with a literal twist. Thumbs up!

1

Spin the spinner on your finger using the steps on the previous pages.

2

Place your thumb back on the spinning spinner while flipping your hand so that your thumb is now on the bottom of the spinner.

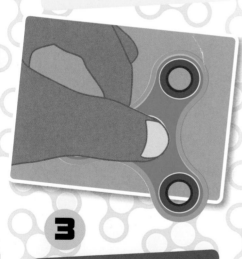

4

Repeat, flipping back and forth from finger to thumb, with the spinner spinning the whole time.

3

Remove your finger and let the spinner spin on your thumb.

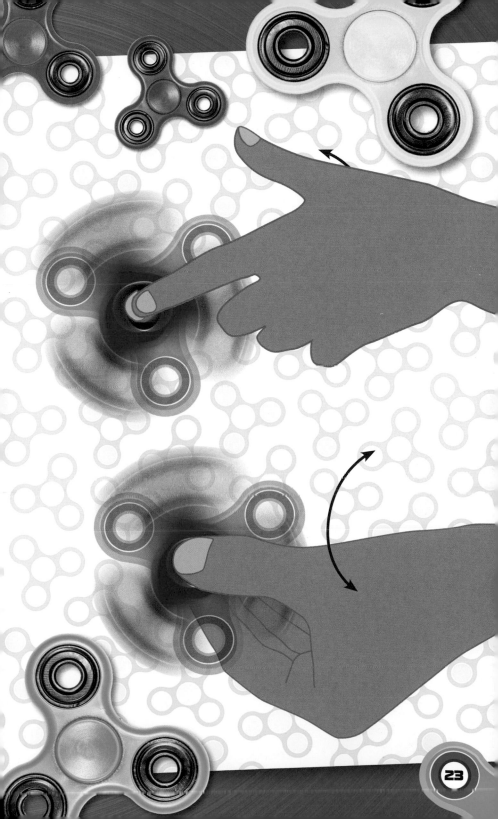

TABLE SPIN

This is another basic trick you'll be tempted to try from the minute you have a fidget spinner. But can you beat your own record?

1

Place your spinner flat on a table.

2

Place the index finger of one hand on the centre piece of the spinner.

3

With the index finger of your other hand, give the spinner a good push on one of the bearings to set it spinning.

4

Remove your index finger and watch the spinner spin for minutes on end.

SPINNER CHALLENGE

Time how long your spinner spins. See if you can get it to spin faster and longer with every go. Record your times here:

DATE

....

....

....

....

MULTI SPINNER
TABLE SPIN

Gather a bunch of fidget spinners to create a tower of spinning awesomeness. How high can you go?

1 Start with one spinner flat on the table. Place the index finger of one hand on the centre piece of the spinner and use the other hand to set it spinning. Remove your index finger.

2 Carefully place another spinner on top of the spinning first one.

3 Place your index finger on the top spinner's centre piece and use your other index finger to start it spinning too. Remove your fingers.

4

Repeat with as many spinners as you can, adding one at a time.

TOP SPIN TIP

This is a great one to do with friends – you'll have more spinners!

CHANGING FINGERS

Let's start building on the basics and move on to some intermediate skills. This trick gets you used to moving the spinner around while it's spinning.

1

Hold the spinner horizontally by its centre, with your thumb on the top and index finger flat on the bottom.

2

Set the spinner spinning by flicking it with your middle finger of the hand holding the spinner or your index finger of the other hand.

3

Place your middle finger on the bottom of the spinner, along with your index finger.

5

Practise moving the spinner to different fingers using steps 3 and 4. If you're feeling you need more of a challenge, try lifting your thumb after each transfer, so the spinner is spinning on your index finger only, then middle finger only, and so on.

4

Remove your index finger.

BUNNY HOP

Let's get serious! You're not here just to pass the spinner around, are you? To start adding height to your moves, try out this hopper of a trick.

1
Hold the spinner horizontally by its centre, with your thumb on the top and index finger flat on the bottom.

2
Give the spinner a good spin by flicking it with your middle finger of the hand holding the spinner or your index finger of the other hand.

3
Lift your thumb so the spinner is spinning on your finger only.

4
Lower your hand for momentum, keeping the spinner flat, then gently toss the fidget spinner up into the air, just slightly off your finger.

CHALLENGE:
How many bunny hops can you do in a row?

30

5

Catch it with the pad of the same index finger, on the spinner's bottom centre piece, without stopping its spin.

TOP SPIN TIP

There's no need to toss the spinner more than a centimeter or two above your finger until you get used to this tricky trick.

FINGER-TO-FINGER HOT POTATO

This totally tricky tossing trick doesn't need much height to impress your friends. Just keep the spinner moving like a hot potato, and they'll be mesmerised!

1 Hold the spinner horizontally by its centre, with your thumb on the top and index finger flat on the bottom.

2 Give the spinner a good spin by flicking it with your middle finger of the hand holding the spinner or your index finger of the other hand.

3 Lift your thumb so the spinner is spinning on your finger only.

4 Lower your hand for momentum, keeping the spinner flat, then gently toss the fidget spinner up into the air, just slightly off your finger.

6

Treat your spinner as a hot potato, and keep it moving. Toss back and forth between your index and middle fingers, or try passing it all the way along from finger to finger of your hand – and back!

5

Now catch it with the pad of your middle finger under the spinner's centre, without stopping its spin.

TOP SPIN TIP

Keep your thumb on the spinner if you need support while you practise this trick.

FINGER-TO-FINGER PINCH GRIP TOSS

Pinch me! There are so many ways you can take advantage of the simple pinch grip and up your spinning game. This one is just a hint to your fans of what you're capable of...

1

Hold the spinner in your left hand, with your thumb on top and index finger on the bottom of the centre piece.

2

Use the index finger of your right hand to set the spinner spinning.

3

Give the spinner a little toss, letting go of it with your thumb and index finger at the same time.

4

Quickly catch it with the same hand, using a pinch grip with your middle finger on the bottom and thumb on the top of the centre piece.

5

Keep tossing and catching, using steps 3 and 4, using a different finger to catch the spinning spinner each time. Try to toss from index to middle to ring to little finger – and back again!

TOP SPIN TIP

Always pinch the centre piece only when you catch, to avoid stopping the spin.

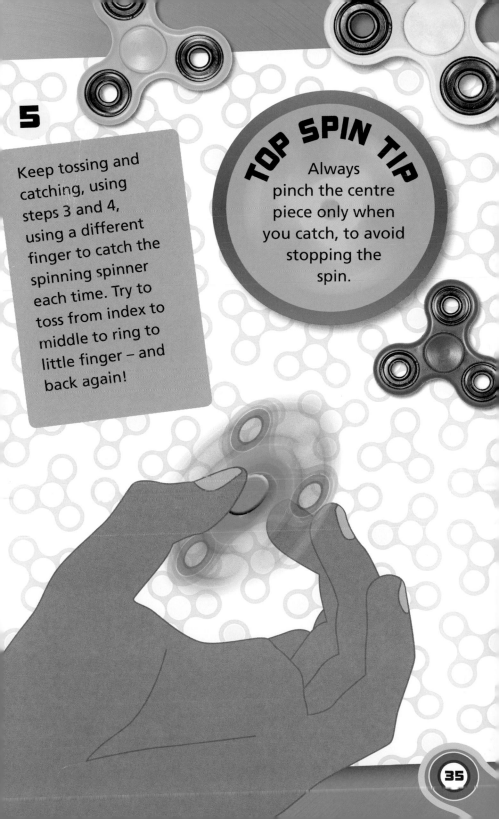

HAND-TO-HAND
PINCH GRIP PASS

Build your skills by starting to pass the spinner from hand to hand. This sets you up ready for the challenges to come...

1 Hold the spinner in your left hand, with your thumb on top and index finger on the bottom of the left-hand side of the centre piece.

2 Use the index finger of your right hand to set the spinner spinning.

3 Use an identical pinch grip with your right hand, placing your right thumb on the top and right index finger on the bottom of the right-hand side of the centre piece, without stopping the spinner's spin.

4

Remove your left hand. The spinner should now be spinning in your right hand only.

5

Practise moving the spinner back and forth from hand to hand, until the spin stops.

SPINNER CHALLENGE

Count how many times you can pass the spinner before it stops spinning. Record your times here:

DATE	NUMBER OF SPINS
....	....
....	....
....	....
....	....
....	....

HAND-TO-HAND PINCH GRIP TOSS

Here's where the challenges start coming! Adding a toss to your pass really steps up your spins.

1

Hold the spinner horizontally in your left hand, with your thumb on top and index finger on the bottom of the centre piece.

2

Use the index finger of your right hand to set the spinner spinning.

3

Toss the spinner up slightly and over towards your right hand.

4

Catch the spinner using a pinch grip with your right hand, with your thumb on top and index finger on the bottom of the centre piece. Avoid touching the outer section of the spinner so that you don't stop its spin.

5

Toss the spinner back and forth, moving your hands further apart as you get better and better.

TOP SPIN TIP

Bending your knees as you catch helps with keeping the balance and spin.

HAND-TO-HAND
VERTICAL TOSS

Let's get vertical... Switch it up with another kind of hand-to-hand toss.

1

Hold the spinner vertically in your left hand, using a pinch grip with your thumb on the front and index finger on the back of the centre piece.

2

Use the index finger of your right hand to set the spinner spinning.

3

Lower your hand for momentum, then toss the spinner up and over towards your right hand.

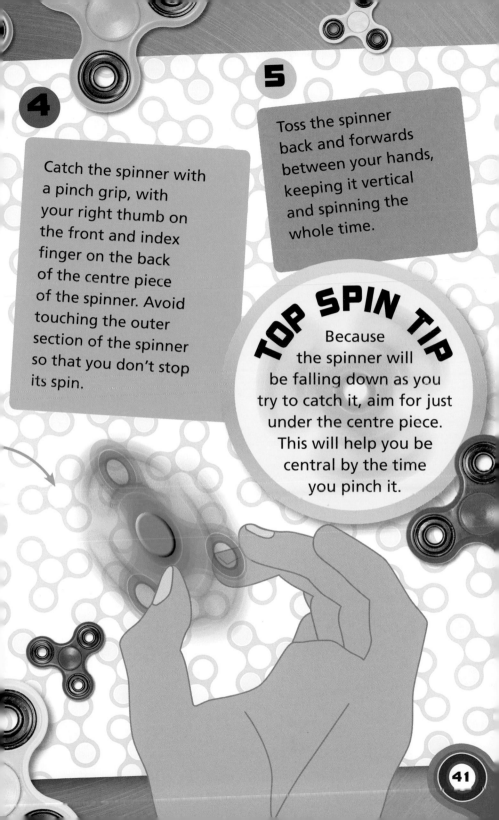

4

Catch the spinner with a pinch grip, with your right thumb on the front and index finger on the back of the centre piece of the spinner. Avoid touching the outer section of the spinner so that you don't stop its spin.

5

Toss the spinner back and forwards between your hands, keeping it vertical and spinning the whole time.

TOP SPIN TIP

Because the spinner will be falling down as you try to catch it, aim for just under the centre piece. This will help you be central by the time you pinch it.

ONE-HANDED FLIP TOSS

How's your coordination? Flip both your spinner and your hand – but don't forget to release and catch too!

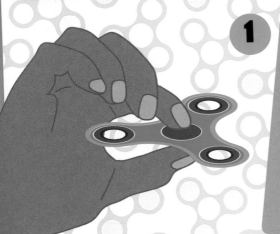

1 Hold the spinner horizontally in your favourite spinning hand, with your index finger on top and thumb on the bottom of the centre piece.

2 Use the index finger of your other hand to set the spinner spinning.

3 Toss the spinner upwards and flip it over at the same time. Let go of the spinner entirely.

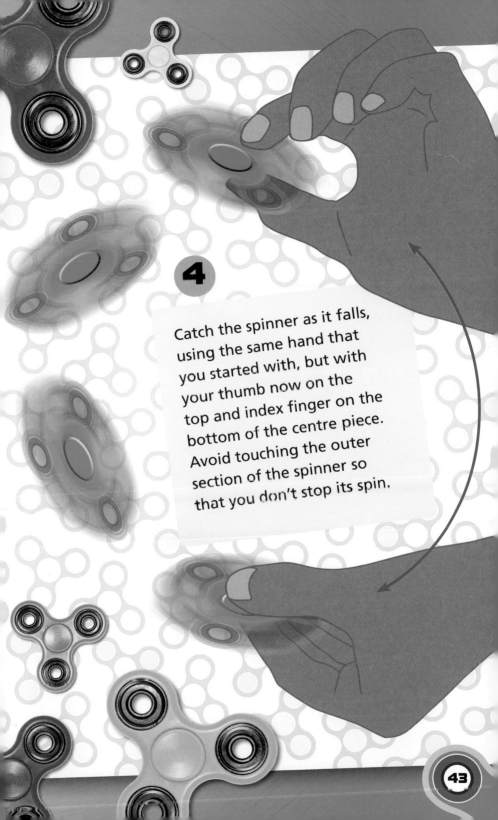

4

Catch the spinner as it falls, using the same hand that you started with, but with your thumb now on the top and index finger on the bottom of the centre piece. Avoid touching the outer section of the spinner so that you don't stop its spin.

VERTICAL
TOSS AND SPIN

Let's mix it up… This trick is unusual in that its spin starts in the air instead of in your hand. See how fast you can get it going!

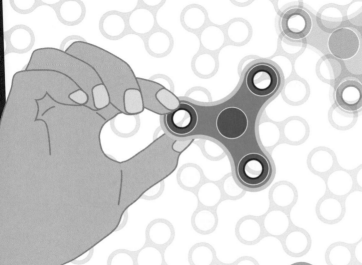

1

Hold your spinner vertically, pinching one of the outer bearings (or edge of the spinner if you're using a round one).

2

Lower your arm for momentum, then toss the spinner up in the air.

3 As the spinner comes back down, catch it using a pinch grip on its centre piece. If you avoid touching the outer part of the spinner, it should now be spinning in your hand!

ON-THE-NOSE SUPER SPIN

This trick is literally on the nose. Just be super careful as you practise this challenge with the spinning gadget so close to your face!

1 Hold the spinner horizontally, with your thumb on top and index finger on the bottom of the centre piece.

2 Use the index finger of your other hand to set it spinning.

3 Remove your thumb.

4 Lean forwards and place your nose on the centre piece of the spinner. Use your other hand to support the index finger holding the spinner if necessary.

5

With the spinner still spinning, slowly move your head all the way back until you're looking straight up at the ceiling, continuing to press the spinner against your nose.

6

When you feel you've got the balance just right, remove your hand. Your spinner should now be spinning on the end of your nose!

SAFETY TIP

Keep your hands close to catch the spinner. You don't want it hitting your eyes or teeth if it falls!

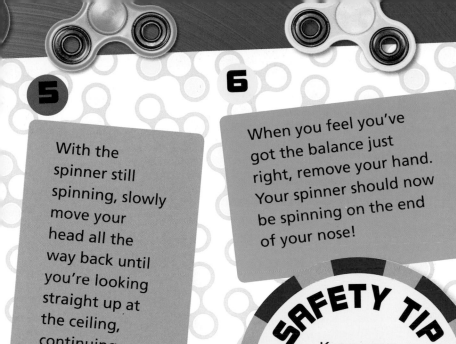

THE GAME OF CATCH

Grab a superstar spinning friend to double the awesomeness. Make sure you are aware of your surroundings – this one's best done outside, where you can't break anything! Check there's no-one close who might get hit if you miss a catch.

1 Stand a few feet apart from your friend. Start close and move back as you get more confident.

2 Hold the spinner vertically in its centre and set it spinning.

3 Gently toss the spinner to your friend, using an underhand motion, keeping the spinner vertical.

4 Get your friend to catch the spinner with a pinch grip in the centre, so it keeps spinning. Pass and back and forth for as long as you can!

TOP SPIN TIP 1

Try tossing the spinner from one of it's outer bearings, without spinning it, and see if it's spinning when your friend catches it in its middle.

TOP SPIN TIP 2

Add a second spinner to the mix, with each of you holding one to start. Can you toss and catch the spinners at the same time?

SPINNER JUGGLING

Prefer to fly solo? Get your hands on two fidget spinners and try out this ultimate version of juggling. Be careful! All throwing tricks should only be done where there are no objects you could damage or people you could hurt if you drop or miss the spinner – outside is best!

1

Hold a spinner horizontally in each hand, thumb on top and index finger on the bottom of the centre piece.

2

Set each spinner spinning, using the middle finger of the hands holding the spinner, or even tapping each one against your leg to get them going.

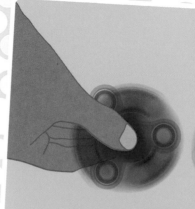

3

At the same time, gently toss each spinner up and towards the opposite hand.

4

Catch the spinners using a pinch grip with each hand, with your thumb on top and index finger on the bottom of each centre piece.

KNUCKLE UP

Knuckle down practising this tricky challenge. Another form of toss and flip, it takes serious concentration but will be seriously satisfying when you get it just right.

1
Hold the spinner horizontally, with your thumb on top and index finger on the bottom of the centre piece.

2
Use the index finger of your other hand to set it spinning.

3
Remove your thumb.

4
Gently toss the spinner up off your index finger. Immediately flip over your hand so the palm is facing down.

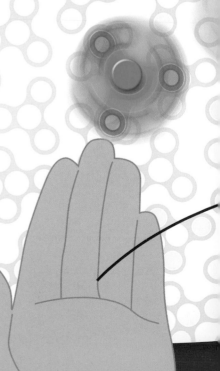

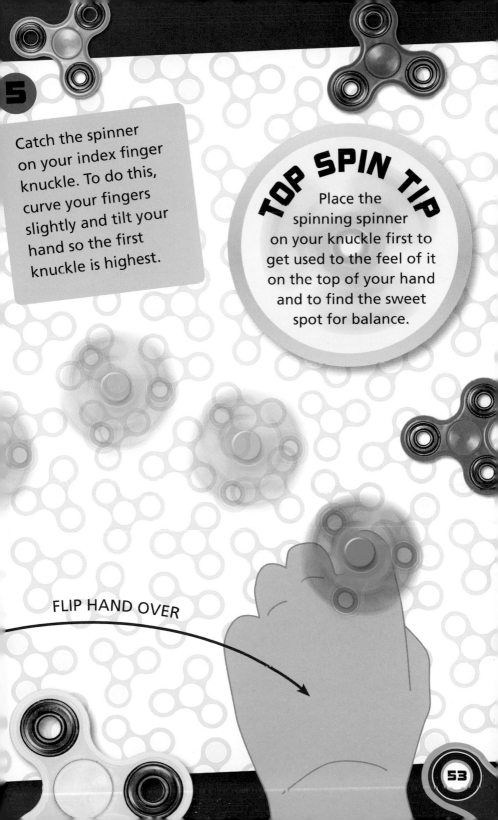

5

Catch the spinner on your index finger knuckle. To do this, curve your fingers slightly and tilt your hand so the first knuckle is highest.

TOP SPIN TIP

Place the spinning spinner on your knuckle first to get used to the feel of it on the top of your hand and to find the sweet spot for balance.

FLIP HAND OVER

HAND AND ARM
TWIST

Add in some body movement to take your spinner skills to the next level. Spin, twist and amaze!

1 Hold the spinner horizontally, with your thumb on top and index fingertip on the bottom of the centre piece.

2 Set the spinner spinning and remove your thumb, so it is spinning on your fingertip only.

3

Twist your wrist so the spinner ducks underneath your arm.

4

Twist your wrist around and up, making sure the spinner is still spinning.

5

Finish with the spinner still spinning flat on your fingertip.

TOP SPIN TIP

Practise with your thumb in place while you get used to the movement of your arm.

UNDER ARM
TOSS

Things are heating up now! Add even bigger movement with this superstar challenge.

1

Hold the spinner vertically in your right hand, using a pinch grip with your thumb closest to you and your index finger on the back of the centre piece.

2

Use the index finger of your left hand to set the spinner spinning.

3

Hold your left arm out and lift it slightly, while at the same time passing your right hand underneath and tossing the spinner straight up in the air.

4

Uncross your arms and catch the spinner using a pinch grip with your left hand.

TOP SPIN TIP

Try to toss the spinner to about the height of your forehead, so you can keep it controlled and give yourself time to catch it.

UNDER THE LEG

Get your whole body involved with this seriously stunning stunt. Stand up tall and make sure you give yourself enough space to practice this safely.

1

Standing up, hold the spinner horizontally in your right hand, with your thumb on top and index finger on the bottom of the centre piece.

2 Set the spinner spinning.

3 Lower your right hand and lift your right leg.

4

Pass your right hand under your right leg and toss the spinner up in the air.

5

Put your leg back down and catch the spinner with your right hand, using a flat pinch grip again.

SPINNER CHALLENGE

Can you pass the spinner under both legs? Toss it under your left leg first, then lift your right leg as you catch it underneath.

UNDER THE LEG AND BOUNCE

Go big or go home, right? Add a little extra touch to the under-leg trick for a big impact. Make sure there's plenty of space around you so you don't accidentally hurt someone else or damage anything nearby.

1

Standing up, hold the spinner horizontally in your left hand, with your thumb on top and index finger on the bottom of the centre piece.

2 Set the spinner spinning.

3 Lower your left hand and lift your left leg.

5 As the spinner comes back down, lift your left knee so that the spinner bounces up off it.

4 Pass your left hand under your left leg and toss the spinner up in the air.

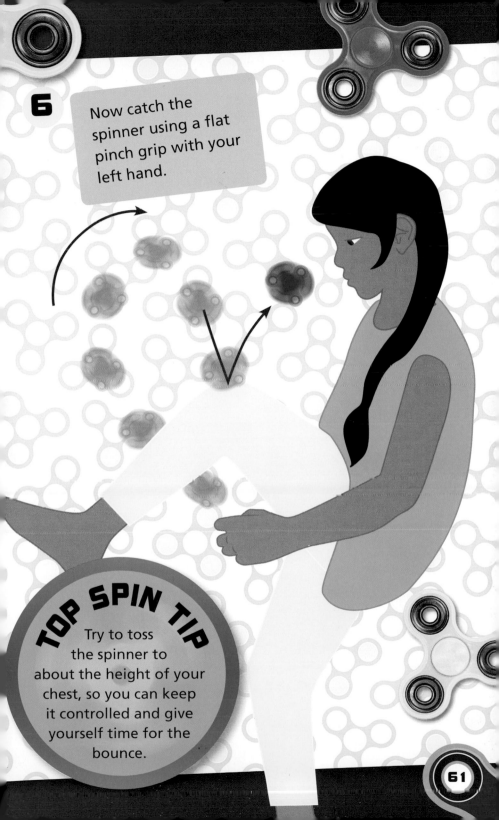

6 Now catch the spinner using a flat pinch grip with your left hand.

TOP SPIN TIP Try to toss the spinner to about the height of your chest, so you can keep it controlled and give yourself time for the bounce.

AROUND THE BACK

This might just be the ultimate solo spinning challenge. Land this and you are the fidget spinner master.

1

Standing up, hold the spinner horizontally in your right hand, with your thumb on top and index finger on the bottom of the centre piece.

2

Set the spinner spinning.

3

Bring your right arm behind your back and give the spinner a good toss. It helps to push your stomach forwards.

4

Toss the spinner under your left arm.

5 Whip your right arm back in front to catch the spinner using a pinch grip.

TOP SPIN TIP

If you're finding it difficult to catch the spinner with your right hand, try using your left hand to build confidence.

SUPER-SPEED
SPINNING

With a little bit of help, you can get your spinner spinning at super speed. Try a strong public hand dryer or compressed air at home if you have it.

1 Hold your spinner with a pinch grip on the centre piece.

2 Hold it under the hand dryer and turn on the dryer OR spray the condensed air towards one of the outer bearings.

3 Watch your spinner pick up speed! Move it away from the dryer or stop the air once it hits maximum speed.

SAFETY TIP

Don't keep your hand under the hand dryer for too long, or too close to the vent. If you're using compressed air, follow the safety instructions on the bottle.

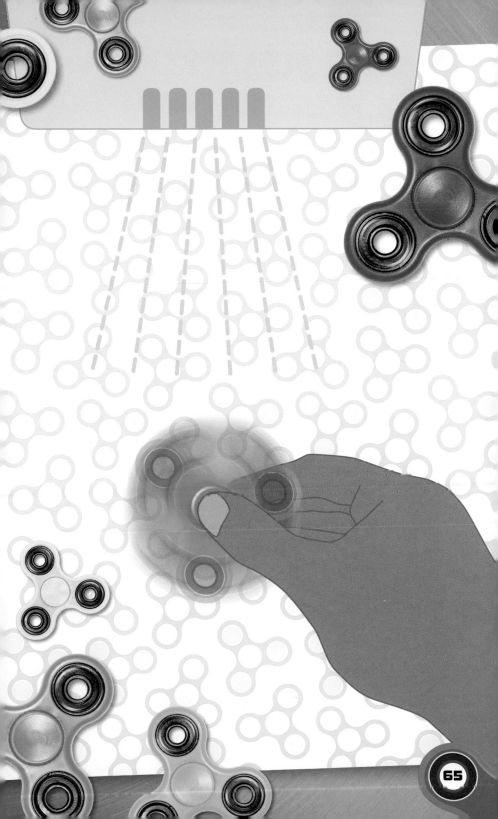

TABLE DROP AND SPIN

Combine a hand spin and table spin for some cool continuous spinning. Just be careful that you don't practise on a family heirloom dining table!

1

Hold the spinner horizontally in your right hand, with your thumb on top and index finger on the bottom of the centre piece.

2

Set the spinner spinning with the index finger of your left hand.

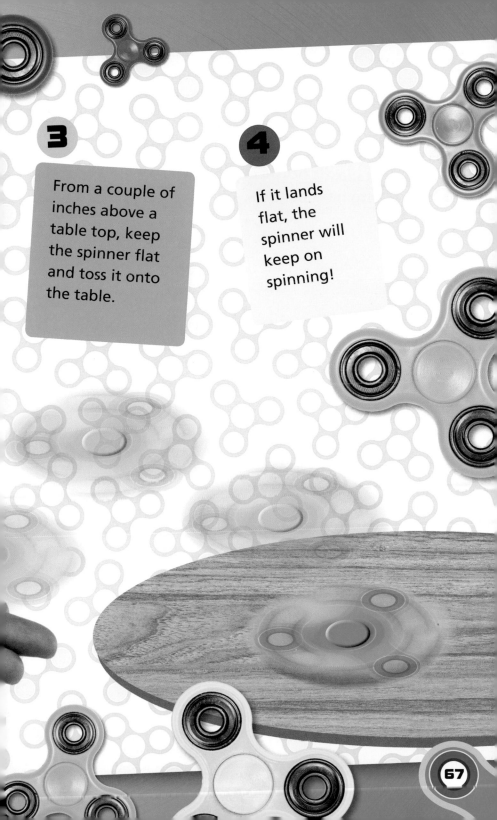

3

From a couple of inches above a table top, keep the spinner flat and toss it onto the table.

4

If it lands flat, the spinner will keep on spinning!

BOTTLE SPIN

This is literally a 'level up' from the basic table spin. Place a plastic bottle on the table, and raise the spinner to new heights.

1 Stand a plastic bottle (soda, juice or water) on a flat surface.

2 Place the spinner flat on top, with the centre piece sitting on the centre of the bottle top.

3 Hold the spinner steady with the index finger of one hand on the top centre piece.

4

Use your other index finger to set the spinner spinning.

5

Move your hands away and watch the spinner spin and balance on the bottle.

TOP SPIN TIP

Keep a close eye on the spinner and be ready to catch it in case it goes flying off!

PENCIL SPIN

For this stunt, you'll need a pencil, mechanical pencil or pen with a flat bottom. You'll also need a spinner with removable centre caps.

1 Pull the centre caps off both sides of your fidget spinner.

2 Push a pencil or pen through the centre hole, starting at the pointy end, as far as it will go.

3 Hold the pencil or pen by the barrel above the spinner and set the spinner spinning with your other hand.

4

Put the pen or pencil flat end down on a flat surface. Watch it spin!

5

Try flicking the top of the pencil or pen as it spins. If it's got enough momentum, it should stand itself up straight again!

BOTTLE-TOP PENCIL SPIN

Take the pencil spin to the next level by adding in another plastic drinks bottle.

1 Remove both centre caps from your fidget spinner.

2 Push a pointy pencil through the centre hole, starting at the pointy end, as far as it will go.

3 Hold the pencil or pen by the barrel above the spinner and set the spinner spinning with your other hand.

4

This time, place the pencil pointy end down, with the point on the centre of the bottle's top. Watch it spin, wobble and balance itself!

PENCIL-POINT
BALANCE

If you've got a pointy pencil and a massive amount of determination and courage, you can master this tricky stunt.

1

Hold the spinner horizontally in one hand, with your thumb on top and index finger on the bottom of the centre piece.

2

Use your other hand to set the spinner spinning.

3

Very slowly and carefully, bring a pencil under the spinning spinner. Place the point under the centre piece.

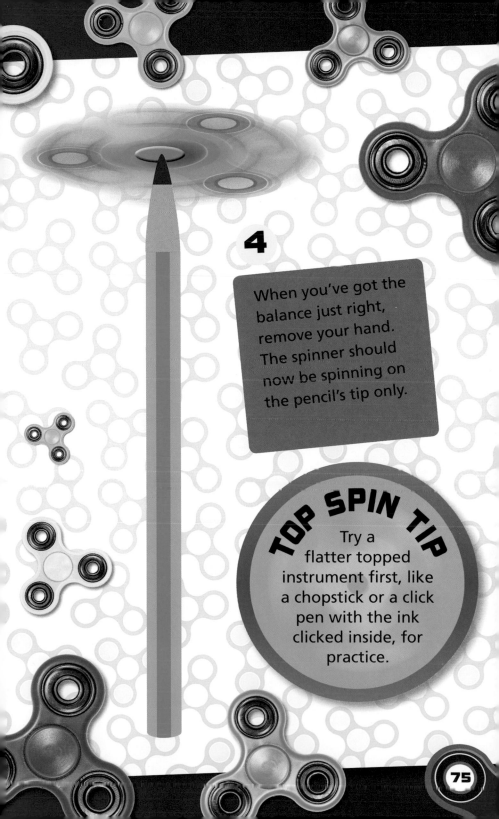

4

When you've got the balance just right, remove your hand. The spinner should now be spinning on the pencil's tip only.

TOP SPIN TIP

Try a flatter topped instrument first, like a chopstick or a click pen with the ink clicked inside, for practice.

STRING STUNT

For this ultra-spinning trick, you'll need a fidget spinner with removable centre caps, a pencil or pen and a piece of string. Got them? Let's go!

1

Remove both centre caps from your fidget spinner.

2

Push the pencil or pen through the centre hole, starting at the pointy end, as far as it will go.

3

Tie a piece of string tightly to the shortest end of the pencil or pen, right against the spinner.

4

Hold the pencil with one hand and give the spinner a good spin with the other hand.

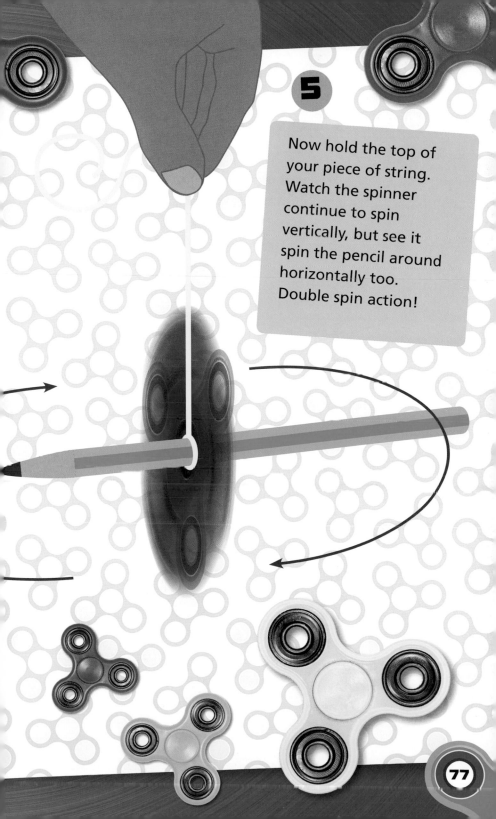

5

Now hold the top of your piece of string. Watch the spinner continue to spin vertically, but see it spin the pencil around horizontally too. Double spin action!

CUSTOMISED
LOOK

Take a basic spinner and make it your own with these simple but striking mods.

1 ### CENTRE PIECE SWAP

Find several spinners of different colours with removable centre pieces. Snap off the centre pieces and swap them around so each spinner has a different coloured centre to its outer bearings. This gives a great pop of colour in the middle when the spinner gets going.

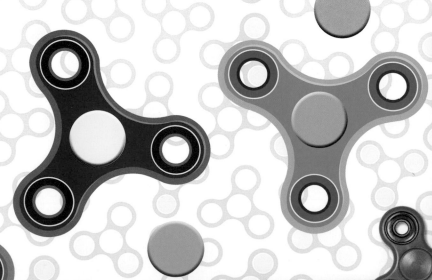

2 SPRAY PAINT

Take your spinner to an open space outside. Remove all the bearings from the spinner. Place the spinner down on an old sheet or cloth. Following the instructions on the can, carefully use spray paint to create cool patterns and colours on your spinner. Let the paint dry, then put all the bearings back in.

IMPROVED PERFORMANCE

Not satisfied with the standard performance of your spinner? Try out these hacks on a spinner with removable centre caps, and check out the difference.

1 BETTER GRIP

You can give yourself better grip for practising your stunts or getting a steadier table spin with this little trick.

Cut a piece of electrical tape about an inch long. Fold the tape in half so that the sticky side is facing out. Place it on the spinner's centre piece. Stick a coin onto the tape, pressing down firmly. Repeat on the other side. Press down firmly again so both coins are stuck well in place, then try it out!

2 BETTER SPIN

This hack is a bit trickier, but worth the effort for a superior spin.

Remove both centre caps from your spinner. Then push the entire centre bearing out. You should see that the bearing has a thick ring inside. Pry this out to reveal the little balls below. Rinse the bearing to remove all residue then place it back inside the spinner. Place the centre caps back on your spinner. Now time how long it spins – you should find it goes much faster and longer than before.

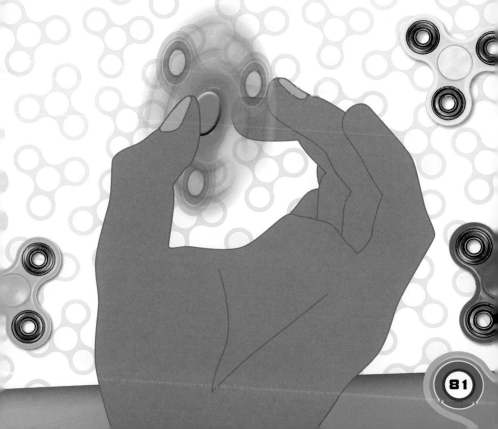

FIDGET CUBE

Once you've mastered the fidget spinner, what else is out there for you? Well, there's the super-popular fidget cube, for one.

This little cube has six sides with different gizmos to keep your fingers, thumbs and hands busy. Roll, click, spin and flip your way to focus and calm.

You can't do as many stunts with the cube as with the fidget spinner, but it is just as addictive! Hold it close at home or out and about, and your fingers will keep themselves busy for hours.

STRESS BALLS

Go old school with this simpler distraction device, but modernize it with your own stunts.

Whether filled with foam, beans or even gel, stress balls are seriously satisfying and stress-relieving to squeeze.

Can you squeeze a ball while working with the other hand? Can you juggle more than one? What about tossing the ball around, over the shoulder, under the leg or bouncing it off your knee?

What can you do with YOUR stress ball?

DISTRACTIONS GALORE

Get your hands on all sorts of toys to calm restless fingers and help keep your mind focused – and challenged!

RELAX
YOUR BODY

If you're using a fidget device for calm, focus, or stress relief more than for stunts, be sure to try out other techniques too. Here are some fantastic suggestions to do anywhere and any time you feel overwhelmed.

1 BREATHE DEEPLY

Take long, deep breaths from all the way down in your stomach, counting to three as you breathe in and three as you breathe out. Practise at least ten deep breaths in a row to get used to the technique, so you're ready when you need it.

2 TIGHTEN AND RELAX

Relax parts of your body individually. Start with your hands: clench your fists then release them, letting go of the tension. Repeat with you feet, legs, stomach, shoulde and jaw.

88

3 EXERCISE

Walk, swim, run, cycle or even dance your way to relaxation.

4 STRETCH

Stretch out your muscles and hold the stretch to reduce tension.

RELAX YOUR MIND

Relax your body, then relax your mind. Try out these calming techniques.

1 HAPPY PLACE

Close your eyes and picture a peaceful place. Consider all parts of it – how it looks, smells, sounds, feels and even tastes.

2 LAUGH

Laughing is an amazing way to reduce tension. Tell jokes, make faces – whatever works!

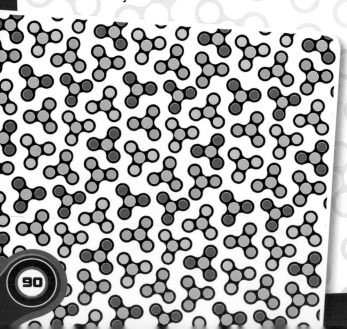

3 HAVE A MANTRA

Recite a positive phrase to remind yourself that you can cope.

4

LISTEN TO MUSIC

It doesn't matter what type – listening to music is a great way to relax the mind.

5

BREAK IT DOWN

Don't try to do everything at once. One small thing at a time makes big things much more manageable.

TRICKS CHART

Tick all the tricks that you've mastered, and add your own in the blank spaces too.

BASIC SKILLS

- [ ] ONE-HANDED PINCH GRIP SPIN
- [ ] FINGER PAD BALANCE
- [ ] FINGERTIP BALANCE
- [ ] FINGER-TO-THUMB TRANSFER
- [ ] TABLE SPIN
- [ ] MULTI-SPINNER TABLE SPIN

INTERMEDIATE SKILLS

- [ ] CHANGING FINGERS
- [ ] BUNNY HOP
- [ ] FINGER-TO-FINGER HOT POTATO
- [ ] FINGER-TO-FINGER PINCH GRIP TOSS
- [ ] HAND-TO-HAND PINCH GRIP PASS
- [ ] HAND-TO-HAND PINCH GRIP TOSS
- [ ] HAND-TO-HAND VERTICAL TOSS
- [ ] ONE-HANDED FLIP TOSS
- [ ] VERTICAL TOSS AND SPIN
- [ ] ON THE NOSE SUPER SPIN

ADVANCED SKILLS

- [ ] THE GAME OF CATCH
- [ ] SPINNER JUGGLING
- [ ] KNUCKLE UP
- [ ] HAND AND ARM TWIST
- [ ] UNDER ARM TOSS
- [ ] UNDER THE LEG
- [ ] UNDER THE LEG AND BOUNCE
- [ ] AROUND THE BACK

SPINNING WITH PROPS

- [ ] SUPER SPEED SPINNING
- [ ] TABLE DROP AND SPIN
- [ ] BOTTLE SPIN
- [ ] PENCIL SPIN
- [ ] BOTTLE-TOP PENCIL SPIN
- [ ] PENCIL POINT BALANCE
- [ ] STRING STUNT

YOUR OWN TRICKS

- [ ] ....
- [ ] ....
- [ ] ....
- [ ] ....

INDEX

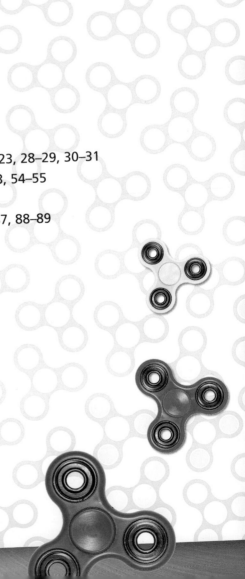

CREDITS

While every effort has been made to credit all contributors, we would like to apologise should there be any omissions or errors, and would be pleased to make any appropriate corrections for future editions of this book.

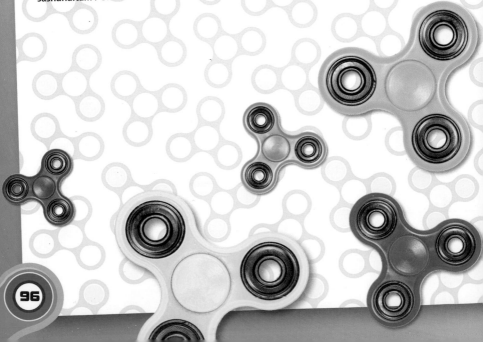